BERNARD INGHAM'S *Yorkshire Villages*

BERNARD INGHAM'S

Yorkshire Villages

First published in Great Britain 2001 by
Dalesman Publishing
The Water Mill
Broughton Hall
Skipton
North Yorkshire BD23 3AG

Reprinted 2005

A British Cataloguing in Publication record is available for this book

ISBN 185568 215-X

Designed by Jonathan Newdick
Typeset by Barbara Allen
Colour Origination by Grasmere Digital Imaging Limited
Printed in China

Page 2 – The now picturesque village of Muker in Swaledale was once the religious centre for the upper dale and played an important role in the area's lead-mining industry

Right – All Saints Church, Thornton Dale; the village was voted Yorkshire's most beautiful in 1907 and is still a firm favourite with visitors

GIVE

Contents

Introduction

It is a tricky business writing about villages. For one thing, you are spoiled for choice. You were spoiled for choice as far back as 1086 when the Domesday Book recorded 1,830 "vills" in Yorkshire. The problem has intensified since, even though some villages such as Herleshow, near Fountains Abbey, have disappeared under the cruel ravages of time. Many others such as Adel, with its glorious Norman church, have been claimed by and assimilated into towns or cities, in its case, Leeds. Haworth just about keeps itself apart physically, if not administratively, from Keighley; so does Captain Cook's home village of Great Ayton from Middlesbrough. Some which were market towns – such as Kettlewell in Wharfedale, once reputedly with 13 pubs to oil the wheels of commerce – have become what everybody recognises as a village as business drifted towards the growing population.

Writing about villages is also a hazardous business because you can end up in the High Court over the issue. Take Usk, in Monmouthshire, for example. It was expelled from the National Village Cricket Championship after beating Werrington, from Cornwall, by one run because it represented itself as coming from a village when, in reality, Usk is a town. A Werrington player complained he had seen a road sign reading "Welcome to Usk, Historic Market Town". If that wasn't conclusive, the judge found that their town council, town mayor and town charter clinched it when they appealed against expulsion. I like to think that this issue would never have arisen if either team had met the average Yorkshire village side. They would have been bowled, not judged, out. But this just shows you what a terrible problem I have had in determining what a village is. Indeed, one of the more enjoyable bits of writing this book has been trying to determine precisely what qualifies for inclusion. (I should perhaps explain that in Yorkshire "terrible" can mean amazing or terrific. One of the highest compliments that can be paid to a Swaledale chap is to describe him as "a terrible sheep man".) The chase has been as futile as it has been terrible, something akin, to corrupt Oscar Wilde, to the unspeakable in pursuit of the indefinable.

My concise Oxford dictionary describes a village as an "assemblage of houses etc larger than hamlet & smaller than town". Thank you very much. It says, slightly more helpfully, that a hamlet is a "small village, especially one without a church". Yes, but... no one would confuse Grassington, the capital of Upper Wharfedale, with a hamlet but it hasn't its own parish church. That's across the river in Linton. A town is "a considerable collection of dwellings etc (larger than village; often opp. to country)".

So to be a village you need to have a fair to middling number of houses and a church in the country. The publication *Towns and Villages of Britain* goes further. It has been suggested, it says, that to qualify as a village, a "community" must possess a school, a pub, a post office and a church. But it admits that this would rule out a lot of interesting "villages" so it is not dogmatic on the issue. My quest next took me to the Royal Geographical Society whose deputy librarian, a Sheffield girl, told me it did not prepare its own list of geographical names but kindly sent me extracts from the Penguin and Longmans dictionaries of geography and a glossary of geographical terms prepared by a committee of the British Association for the Advancement of Science. "Eureka!", I cried, only to stifle it. I found I wasn't much further forrard, as they say in my native Hebden Bridge (which is a town), except that a village has to be a "nucleated" settlement and not dispersed.

The *Encyclopaedia Britannica* developed this "nucleated" theme into the concept of a community: "The village is an intimate association of families while the city is the locus of mass population; the culture of the village is simple and traditional while the city is the centre

CHOCOLATE
LYONS' ICE BRICKS
COLMAN'S
D.S.F.
Reckitt's
WATSON'S MATCHLESS CLEANSER SOAP

Inside the Old Apothecary on Haworth's Main Street

of the arts and sciences and of a complex cultural development. Historically, the village has been ruled by the primitive democracy of face-to-face discussion in the village council... urban government has never been such a simple matter." We get the message: village life is simpler, if not simple – certainly not when Thomas Gray's "village Hampden" withstanding "the little tyrant of his fields" has his dander up. Not to be beaten, I got in touch with the old Department of the Environment, Transport and the Regions. They should know what a village is, I argued. After all, they are – or were – supposed to be the department of communities. "Ah, yes, well," they said. "Basically there isn't a definition." But they got me as close as I suspect I am ever going to get to a numerical one.

"For the purposes of planning, local councils use a population of 3,000 as the divide, above which they may require a certain proportion of houses to be affordable housing," they reported. This accords with the rules of the National Village Cricket Championship: teams must be from rural communities surrounded on all sides by open countryside with no more than 3,000 inhabitants. It seems a bit large to me, especially as the Yorkshire Best Kept Village competition sets a limit of 2,500.

"You're getting nowhere," I said to myself. "You'd better go your own road," which is what any self-respecting Yorkshireman would have done any way. I then had to resist a terrible temptation. The names of so many Yorkshire villages are utterly seductive. You could compile a village curiosity book based on such singular communities as Wightwizzle, Booze, Whaw, Crackpot, Scagglethorpe, Thwing, Wetwang, Mankinholes, Mytholmroyd, Ugglebarnby, Yockenthwaite and, yes, Sexhow. Somehow – don't ask me how – I have put temptation behind me. The choice of villages in this book is mine and mine alone and is based on my concept of a village with one additional requirement: an interesting tale to tell. My only excuse is that, as a journalist, I was brought up to be a teller of tales. I have tried not to tell tall tales. The tales told about my villages are based on the literature, as the academics describe it.

And what a fascinating literature it is. Our Yorkshire villages tell us where we came from and what it was like on the unfinished journey. Nowhere does that better than Yorkshire's deserted village at Wharram Percy at the apex of a Yorkshire Wolds triangle formed by Fridaythorpe and Sledmere, two other villages which appear in this book. Wharram Percy died on its feet, essentially because of poor soil, after somehow surviving at least for 5,000 years. The archaeologists who excavated it over a period of 40 years found evidence of occupation from the Stone Age.

Historical research, archaeologists and the aerial camera have found vast evidence of our ancient ancestors from the top of Ingleborough, one of Yorkshire's great peaks, to the undersoil of York where the Jorvik museum is to be found in the foundations of the modern commercial city. Yorkshire is old England in a big way and was a going concern long before the Normans arrived to wreck it with their "harrying of the North" to teach us some respect. Danelaw gave us our ancient boundary, our old Ridings and a sense of

Ruined medieval church, Wharram Percy – excavations of this well-known deserted settlement have revolutionised our understanding of the development of the English village

belonging a good 1,000 years ago.

It is entirely coincidental that the majority of villages in this book were recorded in the Domesday Book (1086). That was the least of their qualifications when I was selecting them. It just came out that way. But it underlines the continuity of man's occupation of Yorkshire's broad acres. It is also revealing that only eight – just over 10 per cent – of my villages have won the Yorkshire Rural Community Council's best kept village competition. This is not just another book of pretty pictures; it seeks to show those of you with an itch to explore the county what you are missing.

So how did we get our villages? If their Domesday names are anything to go by, they originated in farmsteads which grew, for a variety of reasons, into "nucleated" settlements. The Pennines, Yorkshire Dales and North York Moors are not natural village country. Their remote terrain, soils and climate dictated a more dispersed folk. The Sykes of Sledmere converted their part of the Wolds from wild territory into a bread basket and potato sack. Villages – and estate villages – came more naturally to the richer lands of the Vale of York and Holderness on the East Coast which are more gentrified.

But once Yorkshire began to recover from the waste caused by the Normans and was better able to feed more mouths, the growth in population and other factors led substantially to the development of the pattern of villages we see today outside the vast swathes of land eaten up by the Industrial Revolution – predominantly in the old West Riding and South Yorkshire and on Teesside.

Those factors included the development of hunting stations which, for example, produced Buckden and Hubberholme in the Langstrothdale Chase at the head of Wharfedale and Bainbridge in Wensleydale. Monastic "granges", designed to promote farming on far-flung monastic lands, became Kilnsey in Wharfedale and Ramsgill, Lofthouse and Middlesmoor in Nidderdale. Others secured charters for markets, a cut throat business. First in did not necessarily mean last out. Gradually, trade moved with improving roads to more central markets such as from

Pateley Bridge to Ripon and up and down Wensleydale to Hawes and Leyburn.

Villages grew around resting places along pack horse routes as, for example, at Luddenden in my native Calder Valley near Halifax. They also ebbed and flowed with industry. Not many Dales villages are like Greenhow Hill, between Pateley Bridge and Grassington, specially built to mine and smelt lead. But there are countless numbers in West Yorkshire, the Dales and the North York Moors which owe their expansion or survival (until the flight to the countryside in two-home Britain) to quarrying, mining, whether of lead, coal, iron or other minerals, spinning, knitting, dyeing, weaving and so on. And then, leaving aside Whitby, that cradle of English Christianity, there are the quaint, precipitous cliff-climbing fishing villages such as Robin Hood's Bay and Staithes which long depended on the sea before tourism came to their rescue.

Yorkshire's villages owe their names to a rich variety of old languages – Celtic, Old English, Anglo-Saxon, Norse, Danish and Norman. You get three varieties of stream – the Norse gill or beck, Anglo-Saxon burn and Celtic dacre. The Celts left their mark on the names of several rivers – Calder, Nidd and Wharfe. My own surname is one of the Saxon terms denoting a settlement. Another is "ton". East Yorkshire is teeming with the Scandinavian "by" name-ending which also denotes farmsteads or hamlets. The Danish "thorpe" ending (also referring to farmsteads) is everywhere from that remarkably resurgent old South Yorkshire pit village, Grimethorpe, to Hilderthorpe, near Bridlington.

We have the Old English to thank for "holme" (island), "royd" (river mouth), and "worth" (enclosure) and the Old Scandinavians for "thwaite" (meadow), "toft" (homestead), "garth" (enclosure) and dale which needs no translation. And, of course, you get combinations of languages such as the aforementioned Yockenthwaite, a curious mixture of Old Irish and Old Scandinavian denoting the clearing of a chap named Eogan.

So, we are a mixed up lot. That is less true of our villages' appearance which is largely governed by the county's geology. In the Pennines and

North York Moors there is no shortage of stone. It is everywhere. It dominates the landscape, whether millstone grit, sandstone or limestone – not merely in the buildings of the villages themselves but in the intricate pattern of fields separated by drystone walls. North Riding villages are characterised by their wide grass verges in front of the cottages.

The further east you go the less well endowed Yorkshire becomes with building materials until you reach the East Riding with few natural resources, whether of stone or wood. Chalk, mud and thatch had to suffice, but some of that chalkstone can be remarkably durable as Flamborough's 1674 old lighthouse shows (right). The East Riding's most individual stone is the cobble – rounded boulders from glacial clay collected on Holderness's beach. At least 35 churches in Holderness are partly built with it.

Necessity being the mother of invention, the East Riding became pre-eminent in the history of English brickmaking and it is estimated that nearly 5m bricks were required to build Hull's old walls, started in 1321.

There are, of course, green villages (which may not necessarily imply planning around a green) such as Ramsgill and Arncliffe, street villages such as Thornton le Dale or huddle or sprawl villages which don't have much of a pattern such as many Pennine and East Coast villages like Haworth and Staithes respectively which just climb up and around hills and cliffs. And there are estate villages (eg Sledmere and Harewood) and pit villages, or more exactly ex-pit villages, such as Silkstone which is pulling itself up by its bootstraps. Why, we've now seen in Powys, Wales, the hi-tech "televillage" for people who want to work at home. The only trouble is that it went bust, so we may have to wait a bit for the concept to come to canny Yorkshire.

"The times they are a changin' ", as Bob Dylan put it. Today we wonder where the village will end up under the combined assault of agriculture's plight and urban man's passionate desire to live in the country, though too often without the inconvenience of the cock crow and healthy, rural smells. Yet standing four square and usually at the heart of Yorkshire's rich village heritage is the village church.

They may have been altered, titivated, restored or rebuilt over the centuries. St Lawrence's at Hatfield, near Doncaster, has, for example, acquired for the millennium a new stained glass window which incorporates a WC in tribute to a local, Thomas Crapper, who invented the mechanical flusher. In this and many other ways they connect the present with the past through their fabric and record of the great pageant of Yorkshire life, endeavour, genius and tragedy in their stones, memorials – and glass.

These are priceless jewels in every village's crown. A church at Lastingham, on the edge of the North York Moors, has been sparkling since 654. I believe that, like the rest, it has still a lot of sparkling to do, however Godless the age. It is, after all, the focal point for the community that is the village. The village may be indefinable but you can recognise one when you see it – and recognise them you will as you turn over the following pages.

Maps showing the locations of all villages featured in this book

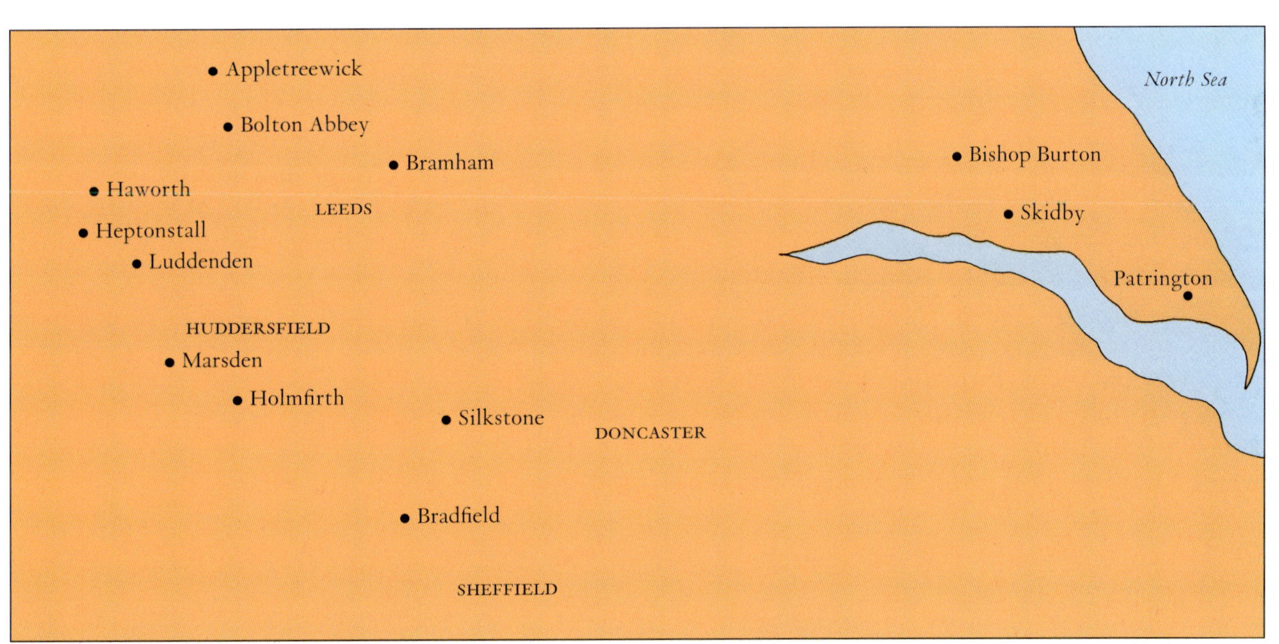
Appletreewick
Bolton Abbey
Bramham
Haworth
LEEDS
Heptonstall
Luddenden
HUDDERSFIELD
Marsden
Holmfirth
Silkstone
DONCASTER
Bradfield
SHEFFIELD
North Sea
Bishop Burton
Skidby
Patrington

Aysgarth

Aysgarth used to be a favourite for our West Riding coach trips. Not, I must confess, to admire the village but the three falls in the River Ure nearby which are one of the many glories of Wensleydale. The peat brown waters tumbling or rushing in spate over the limestone shelves through the woods make it one of the classic river sights of the world. My lasting childhood memory of Aysgarth is of ferns, flowers and foliage – the greenery of the river bank and the gorge and the ivy on lovely old walls. Indeed, its Domesday name, Echescard derives not from its falls but from the Old Scandinavian for "a gap where oak trees grow". It is the sort of place for artists and poets as well as tourists who, when they tire of the sights and sounds, have the benefit of a Dales National Park visitor centre and a collection of 60 Victorian coaches in the Yorkshire Carriage Museum.

You get the best view of the Upper Falls from the Tudor bridge. The village church overlooks it. It has a medieval tower (but the rest is Victorian), and two distinguishing features. One is a 15th century screen, consistently described as one of the two best in the old North Riding, and two richly carved poppyhead bench ends set in a reading desk. They are said to come from Jervaulx Abbey.

Cayton

You might reasonably conclude that, curiously for a landlubber from Hebden Bridge, I like Yorkshire's coastal villages. Nine are featured in this book. But there is a different reason for featuring Cayton between Filey and Scarborough.

It is unique – not because all those Cayton men who went to war in 1914-18 came back. There are three other "Thankful Villages", as they are called, in Yorkshire – Cundall and Norton le Clay, both just north of Boroughbridge, and Catwick, between Beverley and Hornsea – and only 31 in the whole of England. It is because Cayton is the most thankful village of them all: all 43 returned – a record.

May God continue closely to watch over Cayton and its bay a mile to the east as He has done since Caega established a farmstead there long before Domesday recorded the existence of Caitune. Its squat, rather hidden church of St John the Baptist has a Norman doorway to its porch and a north arcade of the same period.

It also has a Stained Glass Centre where the grand-daughter of a Bradford man who opened a stained glass works in his native city in 1884 carries on the family tradition.

S. JOHN THE BAPTIST

Coverham

24 Rather diffidently guarding the entrance to Coverdale where it opens out into Wensleydale is Coverham, a little village somewhat separated from its church. It hasn't much to be modest about. It may have lost a monastery but it almost simultaneously compensated for it by giving us a remarkable son, Miles Coverdale, who translated the first printed English Bible.

The *Encyclopaedia Britannica* says Coverdale translated rather freely since he was inexpert in Latin and Greek. Not surprisingly, this Augustinian friar's first effort in Antwerp left something to be desired so he had another go in Paris until the King of France took against it. He escaped with presses and type and in 1539 produced the Great Bible in London.

Almost immediately he fell foul of Henry VIII and fled abroad. He returned to become Bishop of Exeter where he won golden opinions for his zeal. The Catholic Mary Tudor was the next to take a dim view of him. This time he was lucky to get away without being burned at the stake, escaping to the Continent. When he came back this time, his Puritanism reinforced, he settled for a quiet life of preaching in London.

Only fragments of the village's abbey, founded in 1212 by Helewisia de Glanville, remain in the private house known as Coverham Abbey and in the form of two arches on its lawn and effigies.

The arch remains of Coverham Abbey

Coxwold

Two men take us to the delightful old world charm of Coxwold's broad street, green verges and 17th century houses and cottages. Here, nestling as this village has been between the Hambleton and Howardian hills for at least 1,250 years, we can explore our literary and political history through the lives of Laurence Sterne and Oliver Cromwell. Here Sterne, the greatest humorist of his age, completed *Tristram Shandy* in what he called Shandy Hall (pictured right) as the eccentric vicar of Coxwold in the 1760s. The 500-year-old house stands at the western end of the village and is as odd in design as its former violin-playing incumbent with narrow staircase, quaint bedrooms, uneven floors and even a wheel in a closet for raising water from a well for his ablutions. A perfect setting, you might think, for a brand of zany English humour which runs right through to Monty Python.

Oliver Cromwell's is altogether a more serious tale. Legend has it that his headless remains are bricked up in Newburgh Priory (1145) which has been the splendid home just south of the village of the Fauconberg family since the Dissolution. After Charles II had dug up Cromwell's body and hanged it at Tyburn, his daughter, Mary, wife of Lord Fauconberg, is said to have obtained the decapitated corpse and brought it to Newburgh. The Fauconbergs have resisted every appeal, even by Royalty, to open up the tomb.

The imposing church where Sterne preached from the three-decker pulpit is a veritable museum to the Belasyes who became the Fauconbergs by preferment.

CAR PARK
SORRY
NO DOGS

Great Ayton

The greatest Yorkshireman who ever lived takes us to Great Ayton which Domesday records as lying in the morning shadow of Roseberry Topping, Yorkshire's distinctive sandstone-capped Matterhorn of the Cleveland Hills.

Captain James Cook came to live here at the age of eight when his father became bailiff to the Lord of the Manor. You can't see the cottage his father is said to have built; only a commemorative obelisk. The cottage was transported brick by brick to Australia in 1934 to be re-erected on the first bit of coast he sighted.

But this long village on the River Leven, now being enfolded by Middlesbrough, does retain his school. It is now the Captain Cook Schoolroom Museum, which is one of the joys on the Captain Cook Country Tour. Here you discover the circumstances in which over five years until he was 13 he acquired the basics in a life of exploration which opened up the world.

The good Mr Skottowe, the Lord of the Manor, who paid for his schooling, is buried in the yard of the old church – the village has two – along with Captain Cook's mother and five of her children, most of whom died desperately young. James Cook is also commemorated by a 60ft obelisk on Easby Moor above the village. It is Great Ayton's privilege to honour a truly great man.

Hinderwell

They are not very sure how Hinderwell got its name. It could be Old English for the well by the elder trees. I prefer the other explanation – the spring or well associated with St Hilda. It was listed as Hildrewell in the Domesday Book and it has also been called Hylderwell and Hildrewell. That clinches it for me.

In any case the connection with St Hilda and this wild, rugged coastal village between Runswick and Port Mulgrave is much more romantic.

St Hilda is arguably the greatest of all the gritty women of integrity who have graced our broad acres. She crossed the Tees from Hartlepool in 657 to found Whitby Abbey for monks and nuns. Within seven years her religious community had established such a reputation that it brought together Christian missionaries in the North of England in the Synod of Whitby to chart Christianity's way forward in the Roman rather than Celtic style.

Legend has it that St Hilda went on retreat to Hinderwell in search of solitude and blessed the well which is to be found down some stone steps in the churchyard. That was 1,200 years before Port Mulgrave was built just down the lane from Hinderwell to export Cleveland's iron ore to Teesside's blast furnaces through a tunnel to the sea. You can still see the blocked up tunnel from the shore.

1918

Hutton-le-Hole

Yorkshire is teeming with villages called Hutton which would delight your eye. Most of them come with a suffix denoting a connection with a manorial family or a nearby place or a particular feature of the "farmstead on or near a ridge", to translate Hutton from the Old English. I have chosen the Hutton in a hollow on the edge of the North York Moors – Hutton-le-Hole – because it's one of the prettiest, most higgledy-piggledy, all-over-the-show sort of places with a stream winding its way through it.

On the former Hammer and Hand Inn a lintel, dated 1784, bears the inscription "By Hammer and Hand All Arts do stand" referring to the iron mining of the moors. The village is the site of the Ryedale Folk Museum, a celebration of 4,000 years of life in North Yorkshire with 13 buildings from an Elizabethan Manor House and medieval cottage to a village shop and post office fitted out as it would have looked at the start of the second Elizabethan age nearly 50 years ago. Hutton-le-Hole is the place to go to explore the history of the Yorkshire village and its crafts. They've been working with their hands here a long time. In fields a mile to the south east Mesolithic worked flints are to be found – blades, scrapers and barbed arrowheads.

The Quakers had an early meeting house in the village and one of them, John Richard, a friend of William Penn, founder of Pennsylvania, rode 4,000 miles on a white horse preaching in North America before ending his days here in 1753.

Kilburn

Whenever I take the Flying Scotsman route North through Yorkshire I keep my eye out for the Kilburn White Horse across the Vale of York. This great landmark, 314ft long and 228ft high, was designed by the village headmaster, John Hodgson, and his pupils and gouged out of the face of the Hambleton Hills with 33 helpers in 1857. A charity now maintains it.

At the foot of the escarpment lies the village of Kilburn with its stream crossed by little bridges, a green and a church with a lot of the original Norman in it. And in an old half-timbered house is a memorial to the Mouseman, Kilburn's celebrated son, in the form of a showroom for the woodcarving tradition he established.

Robert Thompson, the son of the village carpenter and wheelwright, was apprenticed to a Cleckheaton engineer. But he had been inspired by 15th century oak carvings in Ripon Cathedral to emulate the great craftsmen of old and persuaded his father to let him come home to learn the trade at the age of 20. He then met an Ampleforth monk who commissioned an oak cross for the churchyard. Other orders followed, his reputation spread and his trademark crops up all over the world. It is a little mouse carved as part of the piece.

The story goes that Robert promptly carved a mouse when a fellow workman casually used the phrase "poor as a church mouse". This symbol of industry in quiet places was for ever after incorporated in his work. Robert died, aged 79, in 1955. He has passed his craftsmanship to his two grandsons.

St Mary's Church, Kilburn

Langthwaite

36

If there is one dale not to be ignored in Yorkshire it is Arkengarthdale which cuts north west out of Swaledale at the little town of Reeth. Its "capital" is Langthwaite with a parish and Methodist church and hotel disproportionately large for the size of the community. The reason is that they were built in the 19th century for the lead mining boom which had turned to bust long before World War II.

The Georgian CB Hotel is named after the CB (Charles Bathurst) Company which operated the mines. CB was grandson of Oliver Cromwell's doctor who bought the land with mining in mind. A powder house from the mining complex remains in a field near the hotel.

In and around Langthwaite is where, above all, you can see for yourself an already rugged landscape scarred by mining which is so graphically portrayed and explained in the museum at Reeth. You can get a clear impression in the dale of how they followed the veins of mineral in "hushes", as the washings and diggings are called, at Turf Moor Hush, 1,300ft long and up to 60ft deep and at the much larger Hungry Hushes nearby. Experts say you will find no wilder or more impressive mining landscapes in Northern England. Arkengarthdale was originally populated by Norsemen and carried the drove road south from Teesdale. Millions have caught a glimpse of it in the shape of the old hump-backed bridge which appeared in the opening scene of the James Herriot TV drama of country vet, *All Creatures Great and Small*. The watersplash also used in the series is not far away.

Lastingham

You don't visit Lastingham. You make a pilgrimage to it. That is the only appropriate thing to do in this tiny, fascinating village in the North York Moors which St Bede found "among steep and solitary hills" in 700. The Brigantes and Romans were here first and there are the remains of a camp to the north east. Then St Cedd was given land in 654 to found a church. He died of plague and was succeeded by his brother, St Chad who established a thriving monastery and became successively Bishop of York and Lichfield.

The Vikings then laid waste to Lastingham and it was not until 1078, when William the Conqueror consented to Stephen, Abbot of Whitby, restoring it, that it again stood witness to the faith. He built a crypt as a shrine to St Cedd and began a great church above it. Sadly, he never completed it before leaving to found a new abbey in York. But his church, comprising crypt, chancel, nave and two side aisles, is complete in itself. It was adapted in the 13th century for the use of the parish and is entered through St Mary's Parish Church.

You walk with the history of two millennia in the rural peace of Lastingham. It is at once a humbling and uplifting place. A village truly of the saints.

Lealholm

The garden in the gorge – that's Lealholm, or "Lealum", as they say in these parts. It has what are described as the biggest rock gardens in England following the winding Esk through Crunkly Gill – a privately-owned nursery paradise for naturalists with a tremendous range of trees, shrubs, flowers, heathers, alpines, ferns and foliage.

But that's only one feature of this pretty place deep in the North York Moors west of Whitby. It has a village green manicured by sheep, an 18th century bridge over the river, an old-fashioned pub, stepping stones across the Esk, one of those village shops which caters for all eventualities, tea rooms housed in the old Loyal Order of Ancient Shepherds' Friendly Society, an early form of social security, a preoccupation with the game of quoits and views, glorious views. It's also on the Esk Valley railway line which escaped the Beeching axe simply because they wouldn't allow it to fall in this corner of Yorkshire.

It follows that Lealholm has a vigorous community life. It even has three churches – Anglican, Roman Catholic and Wesleyan. The Wesleyan chapel has some corbel heads carved by John Castillo, a gifted stonemason, poet, preacher and member of the Lantern Saints, as Wesley's local followers were called because they lit their way to meetings at night with horn lanterns. The Anglican Church is only a century old but attracts a lot of attention because it has an incredibly thin tower only about six feet wide at the base. Lealum, you might say, has everything.

Muker

Muker – a narrow, cultivated plot in Old Scandinavian – takes you to the old mining area of Upper Swaledale in the far north west of Yorkshire within eight miles of the border with Durham and Cumbria. Its connection with mining may stretch your imagination as you admire the grandeur of the fells, the pocket handkerchief effect of grey drystone walls enclosing fields touched with the gold of the buttercup in early summer and the small stone hay barns dotting the meadows. Yet between here and Reeth downstream and up Arkengarthdale came the lead which roofed Windsor Castle and British and Continental cathedrals. The industry's collapse in the late 19th century devastated the area and slashed the population by more than two-thirds.

Muker, lying on top of itself beside a tributary beck of the Swale, became the religious centre for the upper dale 400 years ago with the building of small thatched chapel of ease. This ended the need to carry corpses for burial to Grinton, getting on for 20 miles downstream. It was one of the few churches to be built in Queen Elizabeth's day and eventually became the much altered parish church of St Mary.

They are a cultured lot in Muker which is what you would expect of a place which educated Richard and Cherry Kearton, the celebrated naturalists and photographers.

They have a tiny Victorian literary institute (1868) and a silver band. But their preoccupation is the hardy Swaledale sheep. Mining families supplemented their income by knitting its wool. This cottage industry was on its last legs when rescued by Swaledale Woollens 25 years ago. It has a thriving shop and exhibition centre in the village.

Old Malton

Old Malton and its old stones is the distinct pre-Reformation village next to but independent of (New) Malton on the York-Scarborough road which is tragically becoming one of the most flooded parts of Yorkshire.

It was the site of a Gilbertine priory founded around 1150 by Eustace Fitzjohn and the village grew along the Scarborough road which went past it. St Mary's Church was the church of the priory and contains virtually all its last remains, though its stones no doubt went into other village buildings. The priory's undercroft now lies below an outbuilding of Abbey House.

Old Malton also features in this book because of its connections with Charles Dickens. Buried in the churchyard is Charles Smithson, a lawyer, who lived a few miles west of Old Malton. Between them he and Dickens devised a plot – "a pious fraud", as they called it – to put an imaginary boy into one of Yorkshire's appalling schools of the time. This enabled Dickens to visit some of the establishments for young gentlemen which inspired Dotheboys Hall and Wackford Squeers in *Nicholas Nickleby*.

My Old Malton story takes you from one reformation to the next – from its Norman glories, a casualty of the Reformation, to its role in awakening the Victorian conscience, a reformation of a different kind.

Oswaldkirk

You get no prizes for guessing how the Domesday village of Oswaldkirk, in that rich seam of Yorkshire history twixt the Hambleton and Howardian Hills, got its name. Its ancient church, with much that is Norman on Saxon foundations, is dedicated to St Oswald – and there are two to choose from.

One is the King of Northumbria (634-42) who invited St Aidan and the monks of Iona to convert Northumbria to Christianity. The other is the Archbishop of York (972-92), one of the major figures of 10th century reform who encouraged monasticism and learning. The romantic in me goes for the earlier Oswald but my head tells me it was the former Archbishop whose memory is perpetuated in the village church.

Whoever, this lovely, sheltered place is for ever associated with learning and reform. It baptised the antiquarian, Roger Dodsworth who, partly during the Civil War, compiled the 160-volume *Monasticum Anglicanum*, now in the Bodleian Library. And John Tillotson, Archbishop of Canterbury (1691-4) is reputed to have preached his very first sermon in the Jacobean pulpit of St Oswald's while visiting the rector in 1661. This lucid and logical preacher went on to play a tremendously influential role in simplifying the prose style of Restoration sermons.

Oswaldkirk is some place.

Robin Hood's Bay

Nobody has yet come up with any connection between Robin Hood's Bay – or Robin Hoode Baye when first noted in Henry VIII's time – and that early social worker in Sherwood whom Yorkshire often claims as its own. This, arguably the most picturesque of all Yorkshire's fishing villages, probably got its name because of the power of the legend.

But just as you imagine Robin Hood must have lived on the edge, so does Robin Hood's Bay. Its maze of little streets, ginnels, snickets and red-tiled houses apparently built on top of each other cascades either side of King's Beck one-in-three down the cliff to the sea which runs up the main street. This explains why it is said a ship's bowsprit once smashed through the window of an inn.

The village has known better fishing days but its main business was probably smuggling – and telling tall tales about it. One thing is clear: it never has been the place for Excisemen. It's just built with secret doors, cupboards and tunnels to defeat them. Since 1840, the smugglers have had two churches in which to seek forgiveness. The "new" one is regarded as a major work of G E Street, the architect of the Law Courts.

The narrow streets of Robin Hood's Bay have provided the ideal escape route for smugglers looking to avoid the long arm of the Exciseman

BT

Rosedale

The River Seven tumbles out of Westerdale and Danby High Moors to run south east to form one of the 10-mile glories of the North York Moors, Rosedale. In the middle of it is the village of Rosedale Abbey, the site of a Cistercian nunnery founded in the middle of the 12th century and demolished during the Reformation. Not much remains apart from a tower stump and staircase near the simple church by the village green.

The village is surrounded by splendid heather moors, very steep hills, magnificent scenery and, if you look for them, the remains of its iron ore boom which increased the population ten-fold to 5,000 during the Victorian era. For decades its landmark at the summit of Chimney Bank was a 100ft-tall chimney at the old ironworks on the edge of the moor. It became unsafe and was demolished in 1972.

The first mine, opened in 1851, produced 3m tons of ore over 30 years. But mining was on its last legs when the General Strike of 1926 finished it off. The bed of the railway used to transport the ore out of the dale, running round the rim of the valley, now makes Rosedale memorable walking country.

Fertile valley sides and heather moorland provide a glorious backdrop for Rosedale Show

Sheriff Hutton

Sheriff Hutton looks from the mound of its castle ruins south across the vale to York Minister. This tranquil village in the old Forest of Galtres has had two castles. The first was built 860 years ago by Bertram de Bulmer, Sheriff of Yorkshire, hence the village's name. The second, the ruins of which we can now see, was erected on a different site 250 years later by John, Lord Neville with four large towers linked by ranges of buildings connecting them to provide a court 100 by 120ft. It was one the noblest castles of the North.

Here lived Anthony Woodville, bibliophile and pilgrim and brother of Edward IV's Queen. He was the guardian of one of his nephews, the little Prince of Wales who was murdered with his brother in the Tower by that noble son of York, Richard III. And here was incarcerated a damsel in distress who was destined to become Queen of England in one way or another. The story has it that, while his wife was dying, Richard III ignobly plotted to marry Elizabeth of York, the sister of the Princes in the Tower, whom he held at Sheriff Hutton.

She was revolted by the idea of marrying the murderer of her brothers. So her widowed mother sent her betrothal ring to Henry Richmond who defeated Richard at Bosworth, became Henry VII and united the Houses of York and Lancaster by making Elizabeth of York the first Tudor Queen. In the village's sturdy Norman church there is an alabaster effigy of a boy reputed to represent Richard III's son who died at Middleham.

Sheriff Hutton is a positive pageant of Shakespearian romance and tragedy.

The site of de Bulmer's 1140 castle

Staithes

If you need a parish church to qualify for this book, the fishing village of Staithes is here under false pretences. It has chapels and the Roman Catholic Our Lady Star of the Sea, but curiously no Anglican church. Yet how can you ignore Staithes? Or, at least, Old Staithes which, approaching it from the land, is hidden under cliffs rising at Boulby nearby to 666ft – the highest on the east coast of England.

The old cottages pile one on top of each other up the cliff from the harbourside cluster, clinging all of a jumble to the cliff and cut through by narrow alleys and precipitous steps. One of them, Dog Laup, has the distinction of being the narrowest street in all Yorkshire, just 20ins wide. Staithes is not a place for the overweight.

Nor is it a village for those of timid disposition. Living on top of the cruel sea requires a certain phlegm. Thirteen houses were once swept away and the Cod and Lobster Inn was severely damaged in 1953. The roar of the seas in Staithes proved altogether too much for the youth who was to become our greatest navigator, Captain Cook. His father sent him here from Great Ayton to serve his apprenticeship with Mr Sanderson, haberdasher. By all accounts his heart wasn't in it and within a year he had taken off for Whitby, the sea and eternal fame.

58

The steep cliffs around Staithes provide ideal vantage points for some classic photographs of the village with its tall, red-roofed cottages tucked cosily into every nook and cranny or perched precariously on the cliff sides

Sutton-on-the-Forest

If Laurence Sterne finished *Tristram Shandy* in Coxwold, the great English humorist conceived and largely wrote the work which was to have the 18th century all of a chuckle here in Sutton-on-the-Forest. He was vicar of Sutton and Stillington for 20 years and lived here until, having also acquired the living of Coxwold, he moved there in 1760.

By all accounts he was a kind and hard working minister to Suttonians but inclined to be erratic. Once when his dog started a quail, he rushed home for his gun, leaving his congregation in the lurch.

All prospects of preferment went up in flames when his satire on dignatories of the spiritual courts, written to help his dean, was burned by outraged clergymen. But this liberated him as a writer and the first volume of *Tristram Shandy* soon followed. It made him the toast of London town and it is claimed that a letter addressed to Tristram Shandy, Europe, was promptly delivered to Sutton vicarage.

This incurably tubercular cleric no doubt preached from the simple pulpit in All Hallows Church. But it difficult to imagine he was often melancholy in this gracious, wide-verged village with its fine brick hall built facing his church while he was vicar – and that he found humour its antidote. We're glad he did.

All Hallows Church (right) – the living was held by Laurence Sterne until the vicarage was accidentally destroyed by fire. Sutton Park (far right) – home of Sir Reginald and Lady Sheffield and a fine example of early Georgian architecture

Thornton Dale

Call it Thornton Dale or Thornton-le-Dale, as you will, but it has been captivating visitors for at least a century. It was voted Yorkshire's most beautiful village in 1907 and near the parish church is still a chocolate box favourite – a photo of a lovely thatched cottage in full bloom, the very epitome of England.

The boundary of the North York Moors National Park bends a bit hereabouts, no doubt to include Thornton Dale. It would be daft to leave out one of your Domesday jewels which started life as the "thorn tree farmstead in the dale", to translate from its combined Old English and Scandinavian original.

Thornton Dale still excites people even though it is a classic street village strung along the Pickering-Scarborough road, starting with a green when travelling east with its 600-year-old market cross and a set of stocks. It also has a 14th century church with the rectory opposite, a Tudor hall, 17th century almshouses and grammar school, a mill stream running parallel with the road, a bridge over the beck and lovely strolls through its lanes.

To the west is the site of Roxby Castle, home of the Cholmleys. The Elizabethan, Sir Richard Cholmley, known as the "Great Black Knight of the North" is buried in the parish church. So is Matthew Grimes, a grand old soldier who faded away in 1875 at the age of 96 after campaigns in India and the Peninsular War and helping to bury Napoleon after guarding him on St Helena.

Wath

In Old Scandinavian "vath" denotes a ford. Understandably, there are several Waths in Yorkshire but this – "vat" in Domesday – is in lower Wensleydale just north of Ripon and west of the Great North Road (A1). Its long, wide road and cobbled pavements lead you to the gates of Norton Conyers, the brick stately Tudor home re-modelled in the 17th century, which has known much sorrow. The Nortons, ardent Roman Catholics, took a leading part in the Rising of the North, one of the RC plots against Elizabeth I. In 1569 Richard Norton, the grey-bearded veteran of the 1536 Pilgrimage of Grace against Henry VIII's suppression of the monasteries, rode out at the head of eight sons to risk and lose all for his Queen Mary and faith.

He rode, as he had in the earlier Pilgrimage, under a banner of the Cross and the Five Wounds of our Lord, embroidered by his daughter. The revolt collapsed; he managed to escape abroad but at least two of his sons were executed. This is the tragic stuff which inspired Wordsworth's *The White Doe of Rylstone*.

Then came the Grahams. We are told Sir Richard Graham rode home after the epic battle of Marston Moor, which lost Charles I the North, bleeding from 26 wounds. His horse carried him to his very deathbed where he expired within the hour. The Nortons and Grahams are buried in the old church. Perhaps we should not be surprised that Charlotte Brontë loved the house, She knew much sorrow, too.

St Mary's Church, Wath

Bempton

Bempton without its cliffs would be like Flamborough without its head. Indeed, there wouldn't be much of a head without the shoulder of Bempton (and Buckton and Speeton) cliffs to rest on. These majestic ramparts form the Northern outline of the great white headland which divides Filey and Bridlington Bays.

The crowded, twisting ways of Bempton lie behind the cliffs. Another Domesday village, its 13th century church was substantially rebuilt in the 19th. One curious feature is its octagonal 14th century tower with uneven sides. I'll bet that had the rebuilders scratching their heads. Perhaps that's why it remains.

Bempton's older properties make much use of local natural building materials – chalk and the East Riding's most individual stone, the cobble, rounded boulders from the beach. It isn't the easiest material to work with but up to 35 churches along Yorkshire's Holderness coast south of Filey are at least partly built with it.

One of the sights of Bempton used to be its men swinging from ropes in the breeze collecting eggs from the cliff nests of seabirds which now lead a protected life in one of the Royal Society for the Protection of Birds' major reserves.

Bishop Burton

Even Nikolaus Pevsner found Bishop Burton "an uncommonly attractive former estate village" in the Wolds with its "picturesque whitewashed cottages set back around two large irregular greens". That is praise indeed.

Yorkshiremen have been around here a long time. Some 15 Bronze Age barrows can still be seen from the road as low mounds. The Palace of the Archbishop of York is said to have stood in a field called Knight Garth, marked by earthworks, and in another field to the east is the shaft of a cross which marked the limit of Beverley Minister's sanctuary.

The village church of All Saints, looking down from its mound on the parishioners, goes back to the 13th century. One of its vicars, Peter Johnson (1461), is commemorated with what is claimed to be one of the oldest brasses of its kind in England.

Now an agricultural college stands on the site of the former Victorian High Hall which replaced a hall built around 1605 by Sir William Gee, secretary to the Council of the North. The village owes much of its unified appearance to E R B Hall-Watt, descendant of a Liverpool merchant family, who completed the Victorian Hall and ornamented the estate housing. It also has fine examples of 18th century East Riding farmhouses.

Burton Agnes

Only a Philistine could fail to delight in Burton Agnes, a lovely unspoilt village built around a sylvan pond on the road between Great Driffield and Bridlington. It derives its name, recorded as Burtona in Domesday and Burton Agneys in 1231, to the manorial possession of a fortified farmstead (burton) by Agnes de Percy.

It is more celebrated for its grand houses – two of them, both open to the public – than its quintessential concept of a village. Burton Agnes Manor House (English Heritage) is a rare example of a Norman house of great historical importance. It was probably built by Roger de Stutville near the end of the 12th century and is encased in 17-18th century brick. It is very functional.

The Jacobean Burton Agnes Hall is on an estate which came down from the de Stutvilles via the de Merlays and the Somervilles to the Griffiths in 1355 and finally to the Boynton family in 1654. The present splendid and beautifully furnished house was built by Sir Henry Griffith from around 1600 and there are dates above the entrance (1601) and on rainwater heads (1602 and 1603) to prove it.

He was living in Staffordshire when he was appointed to serve on the Council of the North in 1599. What else could he do but make himself comfortable on his Yorkshire estate? Burton Agnes (and Yorkshire) have been the beneficiaries for four centuries.

The village church, approached through a yew tunnel, owes much to Archdeacon Robert Isaac Wilberforce, son of William Wilberforce. The head of the Hull man who freed the slaves is carved on the chancel wall his son partly rebuilt in his memory.

Flamborough

Our next call is Little Denmark, as Flamborough Head is sometimes called. This is where the chalk lump of the Yorkshire Wolds, striking north from the Humber, curves to an end in the form of a majestic Roman nose sniffing suspiciously a good five miles out into the North Sea.

It is – or was – appropriately cut off from Yorkshire by Danes Dyke, a massive earthwork over two miles long with a bank up to 18ft high and 60ft wide. Unfortunately, the experts are unable to associate it with the Danes. Some say it was the work of Stone Age Man, others his Bronze Age descendants and some even put it in the 7-8th century.

There is no doubt about the capital of Little Denmark. It is Flamborough village itself. It was listed in the Domesday Book as Fleneburg – the stronghold of a chap called Fleinn. Later it was the stronghold of the Constable family. Sir Marmaduke, who fought at Flodden at the age of 70, used to say his family had lived in Flamborough so long that they had forgotten who they should pay the rent to. He reckoned it should be the King of Denmark, so every year he stood on the magnificent cliffs and shot an arrow with a gold coin attached into the sea.

Flamborough grew towards its North Landing when it was a significant port in the later Middle Ages. It flourished as a fishing port in the first half of this century. Its old lighthouse, a four-storey octagonal tower, was built in 1641 and shows the remarkable durability of chalkstone. Its new 19th century lighthouse warns sea captains to steer clear of Little Denmark.

Fridaythorpe

Fridaythorpe is a village from another age – pre-global warming. It was to this high Wolds village and its neighbour to the east, Wetwang, that we *Yorkshire Post* reporters were sent to bring tales of relief from arctic isolation in the days 40 years ago when we had proper snows. No doubt the hardy villagers had a good laugh at our exaggerations. Now Fridagstorp, as Domesday called Frigedaeg's outlying farmstead or hamlet, gets on with providing food for the nation. It is not a fussy place.

Indeed, Arthur Mee, of Children's Newspaper fame, called it plain, even with its pools and green and homes with their distant views. But its Norman church, with its squat tower, compensates. It goes back to the early 12th century and has "an utterly barbaric" (Pevsner) south doorway almost literally carved with any old rope – a rope motif, rosettes, scallops and zigzags. It was restored in 1902-3 by – who else? – Sir Tatton Sykes who also gave it its stained glass windows.

He never solved the mystery of Fridaythorpe: an inscription "This 713 found hear" on a pier. What on earth does it mean?

Hunmanby

If you hear dogs barking in Hunmanby, part of Filey Bay's hinterland, they are only speaking of the village's origins. It was listed in Domesday as Hundemanebi – Old Scandinavian for the farmstead or village of the houndsmen or dogkeepers. A millennium before that a chap was buried here with his horse and cart in one of a number of "chariot burials" excavated in the East Riding.

From the 17th-20th centuries Hunmanby was dominated by first the Osbaldestons and then the Mitfords. But it was more of a market town than an estate village. It had a weekly market until the 18th century and its medieval market cross stands on Cross Hill. Hunmanby Hall, erected by the Osbaldestons, is a fine example (if you ignore the mucking about with it in the interim) of early 18th century East Riding country houses which were noted for their conservatism and lack of embellishment. The lodge and gateway were built of stone quarried from Filey Brigg on which I played as a child – like thousands of other Yorkshire kids. The village's cottages and farms are extensively made of chalk and brick.

Hunmanby can also count a throughgoing eccentric among its clergy. Francis Wrangham travelled England buying books. You couldn't move for books in the vicarage. He even had to build an extension to house them. Their sale after his death in 1842 took three weeks.

CAR
PARK

Langtoft

Langtoft, lying in a deep hollow in the Wolds on the road from Great Driffield to Scarborough, experienced three disastrous floods in 1657, 1888 and 1892 long before anybody had thought of global warming.

On the first occasion, it was half drowned and on the last a terrific Sunday thunderstorm swamped and destroyed several cottages, carrying away trees and hedges and scarring the hills by gouging channels out of the chalk.

On a happier note this Domesday village produced a poet and historian known simply as Peter of Langtoft who wrote an early history of the land up to Edward I and recorded songs of 800 years ago.

It is also what might be termed a Tatton Sykes village. It is one of the many places on the Wolds which benefited from the Squire of Sledmere's tremendous generosity. He gave Langtoft a stone cross on three steps by one of the village ponds carved with scenes of country life and a saint. He also thoroughly restored its 13th century church on the hillside in the last few years of the 20th century.

Patrington

Patrington is the most easterly village in this view of Yorkshire. It's had virtually the same name for 1,000 years for 1033 records show it was called Patringtona. Its glory is its church, the Queen of Holderness, with a spire towering 198ft above the plain. It is one of the finest and most beautiful parish churches in Britain with the grace and style of a little cathedral. A glorious example of the English Decorated period, it was substantially built during the 40 years before the Black Death but was not completed until about 1410 because of this national disaster.

It is generally praised for the unity of its entire concept. Some say the church owes its beauty to the skill of Robert of Patrington who was master mason at York Minister in the second half of the 14th century. The village was owned by the Archbishops of York from Saxon times to the Reformation. Among many other distinguished things, the church is a celebration of the carver's art with around 200 faces of humans, animals and the grotesque looking down on the worshippers.

Patrington itself was a chartered market town from 1223 and its haven was a minor port on the Humber in the early Middle Ages. It prospered until the arrival of the Hull and Holderness Railway in 1854. The haven was abandoned about 15 years later and the village flax mill closed soon afterwards, leaving Patrington to the glories of its church and fine houses somewhat reminiscent of Holland until post-war house building reversed its decline.

Rudston

Rudston has explained itself by its very name for well over 1,000 years. It simply means in Old English "the place at the rood stone" – or stone cross. And there in the churchyard is the biggest standing stone in England – 25ft out of the ground and possibly another 25ft under it (right). Aerial photographs have provided evidence of four avenues converging on the stone.

So it seems that the monolith is the sole visible remains of a Neolithic religious centre which 5,000 years later became the sacred site of the Christian faith that came to Yorkshire in 627. Indeed, Rudston charts our history. Bronze Age barrows and Iron Age cemeteries have been found on its Wolds. In 1933 a ploughman unearthed a Roman house with central heating and mosaic floors, one of which portrayed a voluptuous Venus. Its church is substantially Norman.

It has a large, early 18th century house, Thorpe Hall. And Rudston House (19th century) was the birthplace of Winifred Holtby, author of *South Riding*, who formed a wonderful and sustaining friendship at Oxford with Vera Brittain when she returned there with all those closest to her dead after World War I. Rudston is the place to commune with our past.

Rudston's roodstone – the very old pagan in the churchyard

Sewerby

Anybody who includes a place called Sewerby in his book needs to explain himself. I make no apologies. It's a lovely village, one of the three Flamborough Head settlements to win recognition in this book. Its name has absolutely nothing to do with drains. It was listed in the Domesday Book as Siuuardbi – the farmstead or village of an old Scandinavian called Sivarthr. So there!

Sir Nikolaus Pevsner, the severe architectural critic, raved about its 19th century church, but as a curiosity rather than for its style. "It's amazing," he said. "A Neo-Norman church by George Gilbert Scott." He excuses the architect and blames Yarburgh Greame, his employer, about whose fads Scott complained.

This fusspot was a descendant of John Greame who rebuilt Sewerby Hall on the cliffs 150 years earlier. It is now owned by the local authority and open for the public's recreation. The village itself has a close-built street with "a delightful medley", as Pevsner put it, of cottages and farms dating back to the 17th century built of chalk, cobble and brick. Which goes to show you should not judge a village by its name.

Sewerby's "amazing" St John's church

St.JOHN THE EVANGELIST
FAMILY HOLY COMMUNION
HOLY COMMUNION

Skidby

86

On the road from Beverley to the Humber we find Yorkshire's only working windmill on the hill above Skidby. The slender seven-storey 74ft high tower in black painted brick, was built in 1821 and ground corn until 1954. It then went electric but commercial production ended in the 1960s. It was restored in 1974 and now operates as a tourist attraction, open to the public.

The village (Scyteby) was listed as long ago as 972 and by the Domesday Book had evolved into "Schitebi" whereby hangs a somewhat indelicate tale. The experts reckon it is short for "the farmstead or village of a man called Skyti". That is certainly the explanation I prefer because the alternative – and I emphasise no offence to Skidby – is "a dirty farmstead or village" because the Old Norse for manure is very similar to one of our four-letter words.

Skidby had a chapel by 1225 but the present village church on a mound by the green has a certain rustic charm in stone, ashlar, rubble and brickwork going back to the 13th century, resulting from all the patching up and making do by the church wardens over the centuries. The original settlement of cottages and farms was built along the main street and some of them survive.

Sledmere

No self-respecting book of Yorkshire villages could omit Sledmere (Domesday's Slidemare, the pool in the valley). This tidy, brick and pantile estate village is a living memorial to the Sykes family who literally made the Wolds what they are today. This flourishing Leeds merchant family inherited the estate in 1748 and immediately embarked on the transformation of the house, estate, village and land.

Until then the Wolds were bare and uncultivated. Now they are a bread and vegetable basket. Sir Christopher Sykes ploughed his fortune into the land, planted hedgerows and made roads with grass verges for the poor folk's cattle to feed on. His son, Sir Tatton I, a bare-knuckle fighter among many other things in his 91 years, continued the work of making the Wolds productive, improving livestock and endearing himself to the villagers.

And then came the fifth baronet, Sir Tatton II, the great builder and restorer. He poured £60,000 into one of the last major estate churches in Britain at Sledmere and built altogether seven churches on his estates and restored another eight. He also put up a very fine Eleanor cross in Sledmere which became a World War I memorial. And Sir Mark Sykes, sixth baronet, erected the Waggoners' Memorial to the corps of 1,000 drivers he raised on the Wolds for the Western Front. Have no doubt about it, the Sykes of Sledmere are the very model of a very caring squirearchy. They manifestly put their brass into the community.

The Ornamental Well – one of several monuments in Sledmere

Stamford Bridge

It seems hard to believe that nearly 1,000 years ago the rather commercial Stamford Bridge – Old English for the stony ford replaced by a bridge – was the site of the last victory of the Saxons. Yet here King Harold defeated his brother Tostig and Hardrada, King of Norway, only to march to his defeat and death at the hands of William the Conqueror's invading Normans at Hastings a few days later. I include Stamford Bridge not because of its bewitching beauty but because of its history. King Harold spoke like a true Yorkshireman when Tostig asked him what he would give Hardrada after offering him (Tostig) a third of his kingdom to keep the peace. He said: "Seven feet of English ground". That's the spirit.

The battle was fought around a wooden bridge upstream of the stone bridge of 1727. The centre of the village is dominated by an old red brick watermill, now a restaurant (right). It had two water wheels in the 19th century and was worked until 1964. Now the Derwent flows peacefully unharnessed through the Vale of York.

THE
CORN
MILL
CORN MILL

Thixendale

92

If you want to see a charming Wolds village lying in a lonely hollow in the middle of nowhere at the conjunction of a circle of dry chalk valleys go to Thixendale. It is the sort of place to go to get away from it all. Man has enjoyed the isolation of Thixendale since certainly the new Stone Age for on Hanging Grimston Wold they excavated a group of barrows in the 19th century and found Neolithic pots as well as Bronze Age artefacts.

Not much has happened over the centuries to disturb the routine of the seasons in Thixendale. It once had a blind vicar, Wilfred Armitage Schofield, who inevitably tramped miles to minister unto his Wolds flock. Then came Sir Tatton Sykes II in 1868 to bestow on the village a new church, school and vicarage all designed by the same architect, G E Street. Even the severest architectural critic would say they make a delightful group of buildings.

93

Thixendale is hidden away in a deep fold in the heart of the Yorkshire Wolds and surrounded by the gently-moulded hillsides and poppy fields of the East Riding

Warter

In 1865 a Government report described Warter, near Pocklington, as "extraordinarily shabby", its houses "hovels" with "mossy, mouldy thatch" and "bulging walls". Not any more. Now this green hollow in the Wolds has a pretty row of thatched cottages to remind us of the universal East Riding roofing material up to the mid-18th century.

It generally owes its Victorian appearance to Charles Wilson, the Hull shipping magnate, who purchased the estate from Lord Muncaster in 1878 after he had started rebuilding it. Its roots go back nearly 800 years to an Augustinian priory that was established here in 1132. Only the earthworks remain near the parish church which was re-built in 14th century style by Lord Muncaster. The church is full of memorials to the Penningtons (as the Muncasters used to be) and the Nunburnholmes (as the Wilsons became with Charles' elevation to the peerage in 1906).

Between them, they built a vast Victorian mansion, Warter Priory, around a 17th century country house. It was as impressive as it was unmanageable and was demolished in 1972 to make way for agriculture in its magnificent 300-acre park.

Aldborough

Aldborough, near Boroughbridge, is a lovely corner of old Yorkshire which was once a city. It may have been the centre from which Queen Cartimandua ruled the tribal federation of the Brigantes dominating the North at the Roman invasion. She became a client ruler of the Roman Empire and betrayed Caractacus to the Romans after he had appealed to her for sanctuary. This jezebel then alienated her consort, Venutius, and provoked him into destabilising the North by marrying his armour bearer. He had to be put down by Petilius Cerialis who had sorted out Boadicea.

Out of the original Brigantes settlement grew Isurium Brigantum, as Aldborough used to be called, first as a military camp for the 9th Legion and then the most northerly administrative tribal centre of Roman Britain. It covered 60 acres to Londinium's (London's) 360. The well-to-do lived, inevitably, in the west end in villas with central heating, frescoed walls and mosaic floors.

Roman remains are all around you in modern Aldborough, for long the epitome of an old English village with its green, maypole, stocks, 14th century church, 15th century cross and old houses and cottages. These remains are not just in Aldborough Museum, on the site of the Roman south gate, and other museums in Yorkshire, but behind the town's museum, in gardens, including the garden of the Aldborough Arms, and next to the Roman quarry. Aldborough takes you back a bit.

Roman
Town

Appletreewick

The village of the halls and Yorkshire's Dick Whittington – that's lovely Appletreewick in Wharfedale's green hill country. Originally a dwelling or farm by the apple trees, it was recorded in Domesday Book. It expanded to stage markets and fairs and acquire Monks Hall, perhaps once associated with a monastery, Low Hall, which was restored in the 17th century, High Hall, with stables and a minstrel gallery, and, in Skyreholme hamlet next door, Parcevall Hall, with its lovely gardens.

Opposite High Hall is the village church of St John with small windows and 1635 over the doorway. It looks rather like the houses around it and was, indeed, converted from two cottages. Legend has it that in one of them Yorkshire's Dick Whittington, if not his cat, was born. The parish sent William Craven at 13 to London to seek his fortune. He certainly found it. He became a tailor's boy, prospered under his master and rose after the Armada to become Warden of the Mercers' Company and an alderman of the City. He was knighted by King James and became Lord Mayor of London in 1611.

It seems that the music of the Wharfe rippling over the stones of Appletreewick lived with him for ever. He never forgot where he came from and became a Yorkshire benefactor, founding a grammar school in Burnsall upstream and supporting hospitals, schools and colleges for the benefit of the poor he had once been. Isn't Appletreewick romantic?

Monk's Hall (left) sits, along with Appletreewick's other halls, under the rocky outcrop of Simon's Seat

Arncliffe

You have to explain Arncliffe's geographical position rather carefully. It stands in a high valley leading up to Penyghent, one of the Yorkshire's principal mountains, on the banks of the Skirfare, a tributary of the Wharfe. But the valley is not named after its stream but after a village higher up called Litton. So it's in Littondale which in Saxon times used to be called Amerdale – the name Wordsworth used in his poem *The White Doe of Rylstone.*

All this may be very confusing but it really is worth going to Arncliffe. Its name means "eagles' cliff". And it's a lovely place in a grand Dales setting with its old listed houses built round a rectangular village green. You can well understand why they originally filmed the TV soap *Emmerdale Farm* here. South of it is a Celtic field system with the lower courses of circular or rectangular enclosures still standing. They are either Iron Age or Romano-British. The village church – yet another dedicated to St Oswald – is a Norman foundation but was largely rebuilt in 1841. It grew out of a grant of land by Fountains Abbey to encourage monastic farming. It contains inscriptions to Littondale's war heroes, including nine Arncliffe bow and billmen and "one with able horse and harness" who fought at Flodden in 1513. Arncliffe not only inspired Wordsworth. After staying as a guest at Bridge End, an old house by the bridge, the Rev Charles Kingsley was moved to model his Vendale in *The Water Babies* on Littondale. Arncliffe is an inspiration.

Bolton Abbey

"Where shall we go for bike ride?" we used to ask in my immobile youth in Hebden Bridge. Always, the first thought was Bolton Abbey, that beautiful monument to the Dissolution standing on a bend in the Wharfe. The setting in the well-wooded dale, rising up to the grouse moors, had Ruskin raving about it and Turner painting it.

It was never an abbey but a priory for Augustinian Canons originally founded at Embsay, near Skipton, in 1120 and transferred to Bolton 31 years later. Its gatehouse is incorporated in Bolton Hall, a home of the Dukes of Devonshire, owners of this magnificent estate. The nave of the priory church, built in 1220, is incorporated in the parish church.

The village and the collection of hamlets – Storiths, Hazelwood, Deerstones and Halton East – upstream on the estate, lie amid 75 miles of footpaths, one of which leads to The Strid. This is where the Wharfe narrows into a thundering black gorge. Few have survived their attempt to jump across it. Obligingly, one view of the priory ruins from the village frames it beautifully for photographers through a hole in the wall.

Bolton Abbey is, as journalists say, lifting with stories. There is none to beat the Shepherd Lord, Henry Clifford. Condemned to die at seven, after the death in battle of "Butcher" Clifford, his brutish Lancastrian father, the Cliffords were hidden away in Yorkshire. But after Bosworth and the Tudor reconciliation, Henry, the illiterate, horny handed shepherd, walked the floor of the House of Lords to claim his inheritance, the barony of Westmorland and Skipton Castle. He came to live near Bolton Abbey.

Village scene at the entrance to the Bolton Abbey estate

TEA COTTAGE

Bradfield

Bradfield is at the south western extremity of Yorkshire in that curious little county within a county called Hallamshire. The two linked villages, High and Low Bradfield, are in the high Pennines with their panoramas of wild moors, a mere four miles from the Derbyshire border. Two long entrenchments, one called Bar Dike, provide evidence of man's concern to defend his remote existence here from the Iron or Bronze Ages.

The stone house at the gate of the 15th century St Nicholas's Church in High Bradfield is one of the few watch-houses still left in our churchyards – houses which sheltered those who guarded against body-snatchers.

Sadly, Low Bradfield has known death on a tragic scale. This is reservoir country and the retaining wall of one of them above the village gave way at midnight in 1864. The great head of water roared through the sleeping village and there are harrowing tales of a father seeing his child carried through the bedroom window and a miller seeing his mill disappear before his very eyes. The flood carried all before it down the Loxley valley into Sheffield – bridges, factories, homes and trees – and took 240 lives. A relief fund of £50,000 was distributed among 20,000 people in the devastated area.

Bramham

In Old English Bramham is the homestead where the broom grows. This charming village close to the Great North Road is recorded in Domesday. Its paths were almost certainly walked by Romans en route between York and Doncaster. Its church is Norman. Its moor was the site of a terrible battle in 1408 when the forces of Henry Percy, the first Earl of Northumberland, and other nobles rebelling against Henry IV were literally cut to pieces by Sir Thomas Rokeby's military. Percy's head with its silver locks was stuck on a stake on London Bridge.

Bramham's proud boast is that the gentry have always thought it was the place to live. In this lovely rolling countryside at the lower reaches of the Wharfe they built a positive colony of fine houses – Bramham House, Bramham Lodge, Bramham Biggin, a 17th century creation, Hope Hall, where the great Sir Thomas Fairfax, Civil War general and gentleman lived, and nearby Oglethorpe Hall, which became a farmhouse, birthplace of Bishop Oglethorpe, perhaps the ultimate Vicar of Bray in Henry VIII's day who lived to crown Queen Elizabeth.

But the pride of them all is Bramham Park where I used to play cricket for the *Yorkshire Post*. That severe critic, Nikolaus Pevsner, regarded it as the most remarkable example in England, with Hampton Court, of planning a park in the French manner of Louis XIV. It was created by the self-made Lord Bingley 300 years ago and Queen Anne, who favoured him, fell in love with this grand ensemble of house, gardens and estate. And nobody knows for sure who the architect was!

Burnsall

In my days as a reporter on the *Yorkshire Post*, Burnsall was one of those places to remember when you were doing a holiday weekend story. People flock to this "nook of land belonging to Bryni", as the Old English translation of Domesday's "Brineshale" describes it, to paddle in the Wharfe and generally take the Dales air by the five-arched bridge. Burnsall is usually "crowded out".

It is a wonderful place, nestling by the river beneath moors which rise to 1,600ft. It also has a marvellous church which I last saw being florally decorated for Easter. Somehow, I felt transported back centuries amid the bustle. Perhaps it was because St Wilfrid's is rich in Anglo-Saxon fragments, the only three hogback grave covers of Viking vintage discovered in the Dales and what Arthur Mee described as "an extraordinarily crude" 11th century font.

It was "butified" in 1612, as an inscription puts it. That work would have been paid for by Yorkshire's Dick Whittington, Sir William Craven, who, as I have already recorded, set out with next to nothing from neighbouring Appletreewick and became Lord Mayor of London. He also founded in 1602 Burnsall's grammar school, just south of the church, which looks like a manor house with its mullioned windows.

III

Giggleswick

It is entirely untrue that Giggleswick features in this book because of its name. Its appearance on road signs around Settle may over the years have generated a million smiles among day trippers. But it is no laughing matter. The "Ghigeleswic" recorded in Domesday Book translates from the Old English as the "dwelling or (dairy) farm of a man called Gikel or Gichel" which is thought to be the short form of the biblical name Judichael.

This grey village across the river from Settle is set against a magnificent mountainous limestone backdrop of Ingleborough and Penyghent. It is mainly famous for its public school whose severe 16th and 17th century buildings are grouped to the west of it. It was granted a royal charter in 1553 and its observatory was used by the Astronomer Royal in 1927 to observe an eclipse of the sun. The magnificent chapel, with its rich interior, stands alone looking down on school and village and is identifiable for miles around by its copper dome (right). The chapel was the gift of Walter Morrison, a curious millionaire who for 64 years lived at Malham Tarn, to which he attracted Ruskin, Charles Darwin and Kingsley who started writing *The Water Babies* there.

The village has some 17th and 18th century cottages typical of the Craven area and about a mile away an ebbing and flowing well which has risen and fallen irregularly over the centuries through some siphoning effect in the limestone. Its mostly 15th century church is dedicated to St Akelda who is believed to have been a Saxon saint strangled for her faith. A portrait plaque remembers Dr George Birkbeck, a son of Settle who built up a fashionable London practice as a physician, went into adult education in Glasgow and founded that great self-improvement movement, the Mechanics' Institutes.

Grassington

Grassington in Wharfedale was recorded as "Ghersintone" – ie grazing farm – in Domesday but it had been the haunt of Ancient Britons long before then. We know that from the remains of a proliferation of Bronze and Iron Age barrows, camps and settlements found in its limestone surroundings as well as evidence of Roman lead mining. It has probably the finest pattern of Iron Age field banks or "lynchets" above it.

This early settlement, 700ft up in the Pennines, grew on the back of mineral mining and a well-trodden monastic route into today's immensely popular tourist haunt with an "exceptionally attractive" village street, as the not easily impressed Nikolaus Pevsner, the architectural authority, described it. It was understandably chosen as the HQ for the Yorkshire Dales National Park. Its Upper Wharfedale Museum of farming and industry is to be found in The Square from which lead quaint streets lined by interesting old buildings. Tucked away in one of them is the Old Hall which goes back to the 13th century.

I have been looking in on this capital of Upper Wharfedale, as it is known, and its ancient Grass Wood for over 60 years. This is Northern England in all its glory, ancient and modern. Yet curiously it doesn't have a church. Its spiritual needs are catered for by the one in nearby Linton. But it once had a theatre in an attic. The famous Edmund Kean performed there in 1807 on a stage lit by six candles. It also launched Harriet Mellon, the actress who married Thomas Coutts, then the richest man in London.

Haworth

Arthur Mee, of Children's Newspaper fame, found Haworth a grim, melancholy and depressing place. He probably went there on one of those dark, storm-tossed, rain-lashed days the Pennines so often experience. It is true that its people used to die like flies from consumption. It is the case that the Brontë sisters – Charlotte, Emily and Anne – experienced much sadness and isolation in their strange, death-ridden parsonage presided over by their widowed father, Patrick Prunty (as he started life in Ireland). Their ne'er-do-well sot of a brother gone bad, Branwell, caused them much anguish, too.

But, black though the millstone grit is hereabouts, I have always found it an inspiring place. It was out of this unlikely propagating shed on the edge of wild peat moors that genius blossomed not once but thrice. The sisters' novels are among the finest in the English language.

And I defy anybody to stand at Top Withens, reputedly the model for *Wuthering Heights* high above the literary shrine below, to which I have often climbed from Hebden Bridge on the other side of the watershed, to be unmoved by the bleak grandeur of it all. So let us rejoice in Haworth and its steep cobbled street rising up to the church and parsonage where you can see how the Brontës lived.

They come here by the thousand to pay homage. There are even direction signs in Japanese. The world comes to celebrate the triumph of the Brontë sisters' spirit over their many adversities. So, dispiriting though the Brontë commercialisation may be, Haworth is no place for anti-depressants but for toasts to exceptional triumph.

RESTAURANT

Heptonstall

I was brought up on the south-facing slope of the hill on top of which sits the ancient millstone grit village of Heptonstall, Old English for the farmstead where the wild rose grows. This western rampart of West Yorkshire, surprisingly not mentioned in Domesday, looks down on three valleys – the Calder, Colden and Hebden, with its incomparable Hardcastle Crags.

John Wesley, a frequent visitor, said he could not conceive of anything more delightful than its countryside. In those pre-industrial days the steep, wooded valleys were impenetrable swamps. The settlements were on the shelves of land on the rim of the valleys below the moors. The steep, winding cobbled street of weavers' cottages climbs up the hill to a matchless Pennine panorama. It is claimed that Paulinus toiled up the precipitous packhorse route called the Buttress out of what is now my native Hebden Bridge to preach here 1,300 years ago when he was trying to convert King Edwin to Christianity.

Its old 13th century St Thomas a Becket church was dismantled and left a ruin when the lofty new one was built next to it in 1854. Lying in its churchyard, apart from my grandfather, is poet Sylvia Plath, first wife of the late Poet Laureate, Ted Hughes, who began life down the Calder Valley at Mytholmroyd. But Heptonstall is chiefly known for its octagonal Wesleyan chapel, one of the oldest in the world, John Wesley laid its foundation stone in 1764. Not surprisingly in this staunchly non- conformist area, Heptonstall was the bastion of Parliament in a Royalist West Yorkshire during the Civil War. The Roundheads bloodily repulsed the Cavaliers in set battle on my boyhood hillside on November 1, 1643.

Holmfirth

It is a joke in my family that the sun always shines in Holmfirth, south of Huddersfield in the deep-cleft Holme Valley. "Another lovely day", we used to say in unison when another episode of *Last of the Summer Wine* came on the TV screen on Sunday evenings. I can't ever remember it raining on dear old Compo, still less Nora Batty. But then it wouldn't dare dampen Nora's curlers, would it? Sadly, it rained in 1852 when the Bilberry reservoir burst and claimed 81 lives as the head of water tore through the valley. It was one of five serious floods Holmfirth has experienced, starting in 1777. That claimed three lives as did one in 1944.

Holmfirth is an example of what TV can do to you. It has converted a declining stone-built wool village into a tourist haunt. They devour butties in Sid's Cafe and gaze at Nora's cottage, so typical of thousands of millworkers' homes in the West Riding, built on top of each other with a great array of steps, iron railings, verandahs and caustic soda-scoured paving stones overlooking streams or canals.

The village also has the Holmfirth Postcard Museum, including the saucy seaside variety produced by Bamforths in the first half of the 20th century, and the Ashley Jackson Galleries. Ashley Jackson, the TV art teacher, has a love affair with Yorkshire's moors and the Dalesman has published a superb book of his most personal watercolours. They are, I can testify, a joy to own. The village has a large 18th century parish church close to the river, an ornate Methodist church and the former Town Hall with a classical façade. Holmfirth may have known more substantial days but never more popular ones.

Hubberholme

I'm not sure Hubberholme strictly qualifies as a village, even though it has a celebrated church and a pub. It's tiny as villages go but you can't ignore it. For one thing, J B Priestley, one of Yorkshire's literary lions, would turn in his grave if I did. He loved it. It was originally the homestead of a woman called Hunburh, according to the Old English translation of its Domesday name, and lies in Langstrothdale, as Upper Wharfedale is called.

The area used to be a hunting chase and St Michael's began life as a forest chapel which the Earl of Northumberland gave to the monks at Coverham in 1241. It was a mere chapel of ease for Arncliffe in the next dale with no rights of burial. So – and this was typical of the rigours of early Dales' Christians – the dead had to be carried to Arncliffe, five miles over the top of Old Cote Moor and eight by the easier route. History records how eight bearers once nearly perished in snowdrifts and how the swollen Wharfe swept a body from other mourners' grasp. Today the church, with its Norman tower, is a rustic example of the Pennine Perpendicular style with a rough interior and one great treasure: one of two rood lofts left in Yorkshire. It is dated 1558. Rood lofts – balconies to support a crucifix – were torn out during the Reformation to eradicate all traces of popery. Hubberholme's no doubt survives because of its remoteness. Its New Year Day Parliament also continues in the pub. The vicar and churchwardens meet in a room called the House of Lords and farmers in the bar (the Commons) and, egged on by the vicar, bid to rent the field behind the church for the coming year.

Ingleton

The translation of its Old English name which pre-dates Domesday tells you everything you need to know about Ingleton's geographical position. "Inglestune", as it was originally called, means the farmstead near the hill or peak. Ingleton stands on the Settle-Kendal road in the shadow of Ingleborough (2,372ft), one of the Yorkshire Dales' three peaks. St Mary's Church has one of the best Norman fonts in the old West Riding.

This is classic limestone walking, caving and waterfall country. It is the land of the pots which swallow mountain streams into caves such as the famous White Scar Caves. These were discovered in 1923 and, like Ingleborough Cave, have a wonderful display of glittering stalactites and stalagmites. The waterfalls fall thick and fast in the valleys of the Kingsdale Beck and the River Greta.

Above all these fascinations lies, literally, the *piece de resistance* right on top of the millstone grit cap which protects the plateau summit of Ingleborough. Here you find England's most lofty Iron Age hill fort covering 15 acres with a 1,000ft pear-shaped stone rampart, now sadly plundered for cairn building. It was something more than just a bolt hole, though they had only rainwater for drinking, for there is evidence of circular footings for huts. One thing is for sure: the Brigantes were a hardy lot.

Kettlewell

You could reasonably be excused for thinking Kettlewell had its ancestry among Parisian courtesans when you read its entry in Domesday. It is "Cheteleuuelle" which translates prosaically from the Old Scandinavian as "spring or stream in a deep valley". This has it about right. It's in a gorge along the upper reaches of Wharfedale and lies in the shadow of Great Whernside. Its fells provide dramatic evidence of glacial scouring.

In several ways, solid stone-built Kettlewell is at the meeting of ways – of packhorse routes and the boundaries of the lands of three old religious houses – Bolton Priory and Fountains and Coverham Abbeys. As such, it once occupied a more vital economic position than now. It was granted a market charter in the 13th century and is said to have had 13 pubs to lubricate the commerce. It fell by the wayside when trade followed the population south and east.

Now it is hugely patronised by walkers and day trippers. The village itself is a conservation area. It also offers an adventurous drive through a 15th century hunting reserve up Park Rash and over the top into lovely Coverdale. This was part of the old, testing coaching route from London to Richmond which ran long after Wensleydalers tried to keep Wharfedalers at bay with the Tor Dyke earthwork on the watershed.

Linton

128

Whenever you come across a Linton it signifies that flax was grown there. And, sure enough, they used to grow and spin flax around the edge of what used to be a lake on the flats across the Wharfe from Grassington where the beautiful village of Linton in Craven stands. No more. Linton is now an unspoiled delight to behold. Its green is crossed by a stream that can be negotiated by rudimentary clapper bridge, 14th century packhorse bridge, road bridge, stepping stones and a ford. When the packhorse bridge was repaired in the 17th century Dame Elizabeth Redmayne got her own back on farmers who wouldn't contribute to the cost. She had a parapet added to stop carts going over it. Naughty.

Richard Fountaine was nice. He endowed a hospital and almshouses for "indigent women" in 1721 which stand on the green along with lovely cottages, the 16th century Linton Hall and White Abbey House where Halliwell Sutcliffe lived until his death in the year I was born. His Pennine romances reek of peat, privation and pride.

Perhaps the jewel in Linton's crown is its marvellous church standing low and apart from the village by the Wharfe overlooking Linton Falls. St Michael and All Angels is one of the older churches in the Dales with Norman elements. There is some speculation that the original was built before the Conquest on a pagan site. The present church was for the manor of Linton and served Grassington, Hebden and Threshfield as well. Its lord, Sir John le Gras appointed three of his relatives in succession as parson. Then the right to appoint a rector was divided so Linton had two until 1866. Instead of a tower, the church has a distinctive little, square bell-turret.

Luddenden

130

No cub reporter of a local weekly newspaper ever forgets the first district for which he is given responsibility. Mine was the Luddenden Valley which cuts north out of Calderdale just west of Halifax. Every Monday afternoon I cycled about ten miles from and back to Hebden Bridge via the steep, winding ways of Luddenden village collecting news.

This millstone grit settlement, hemmed in by hills and gathered around the early 19th century St Mary's parish church by the stream, is not old as villages go in this book. It was a resting point on the packhorse route between Yorkshire and Lancashire. Its Lord Nelson Inn, dated 1654, no doubt refreshed the travellers. It also too often detained Branwell Brontë when he was stationmaster at Luddenden Foot where the Calder and Luddenden Valleys meet. Its wool spinning was a cottage industry until the Murgatroyds built the now largely derelict Oats Royd Mills looking down on the village.

They were also responsible for Kershaw House (1650) which is a fine example of so-called Halifax Houses and one of the many splendid 17th century properties which are dotted around the valley. There's not much industry left now. But Luddenden briefly found fame when it became the film set for Thora Hird's TV comedy *In Loving Memory* based on an undertaker's business. It should also be recorded it has a wonderfully-kept churchyard. I know because my wife's sisters and their husbands are buried in it close by the stream. In spring, it would inspire Gray to write another elegy.

Marsden

Marsden is one of those villages you either depart from into utter darkness or burst upon out of inky blackness. It is in the high boundary valley – the probable meaning of its name first noted in the 13th century – where the trans-Pennine railway and narrowboat canal disappear into Standedge Tunnels on the way to Lancashire three miles away. Up above lie vast brown, brooding moors where the merlin flies and remains of Middle Stone Age man are to be found. This forbidden terrain was crossed for centuries by long packhorse trains wending their way in and out of Yorkshire, Lancashire and Derbyshire and the village still has two packhorse bridges to show for it.

Marsden is undoubtedly a mill village. You cannot miss its factories among the millstone streets. It was built on the wool trade. It has also known desperate times. The Luddites were very active up here. They saw machinery as a threat to their livelihoods so they took hammers to the cropping frames – "Enochs", as they were called – made by Enoch and James Taylor in Marsden. In another Luddite incident, an outspoken local mill owner, William Horsfall was shot dead. Marsden is very much part of our industrial revolution. It also has the distinction of giving birth to Henrietta Thompson, mother of General James Wolfe who conquered Quebec. In a letter to her, the general said that all her life she had been "a match for all the beauties". I've no doubt Marsden's bracing moorland air helped her complexion.

Where the canal goes under the moor to Lancashire at Marsden

HUDDERSFIELD NARROW · BRITAINS HIGHEST CANAL
CRUISE ENQUIRIES
TEL. 0161 339 1332
P10

Middlesmoor

The Yorkshire Dales offer a wonderful choice of places to get away from it all. But Middlesmoor at the head of Nidderdale, next stop the summit of Little Whernside, takes some beating. Its lovely stone church and cottages are, in fact, tucked away on the rise which separates the Nidd from How Stean Beck. It is a land of panoramas and skylarks and a peace which these days passeth all understanding.

Middlesmoor almost certainly grew out of a farmstead established around a Byland Abbey monastic grange. It expanded on quarrying and mining. But its origins in the legend are altogether more romantic. It is associated with St Chad, the patron saint of its church, which has, indeed, an ancient St Chad Cross, and there are those which claim that its lofty position and curving churchyard walls suggest that a pagan site was appropriated for Christian worship. You are certainly closer to God in Middlesmoor, 1,000ft up in the hills, than in most Yorkshire villages.

In the days when we had hard winters, Middlesmoor often used to be snowed up. But imagine the life the early settlers lived up here. Until 1484, when they were granted a chapel, corpses for burial and babies for christening had to be taken 10 miles to Kirkby Malzeard. We don't know we're born, do we?

Ramsgill

The last time I visited Ramsgill the wild geese put on a tremendous display for me. They took off *en masse*, as if for an intensive bombing raid, leaving the surface of Gouthwaite water, just below the village, mightily disturbed. Bradford Corporation's reservoir, built about 100 years ago, has become a birdwatcher's paradise. The osprey and golden eagle have been seen there. So you never know your luck.

The village around its little green captivated us when my wife and I spent an extremely well-fed week at the creeper-clad Yorke Arms which looks on to it. The hotel was built as a shooting lodge for the Yorke family which used to be a power in upper Nidderdale. There seems little doubt that, like so many settlements in the higher reaches of the dale, Ramsgill grew out of a monastic grange, in this case associated with Byland Abbey. Remains of its chapel can be found in the churchyard. It was noted in 1198 as Ramesgile which confuses the experts. Some say it means the "ravine of the ram"; others "the place where wild garlic grows". The former sounds the more likely.

The village is almost certainly smaller than it was in its pomp. The locals reported a century ago that a score or more of thatched homesteads had been abandoned over the years. One of its sons, Eugene Aram, became a notable student of languages. Unfortunately, in 1758 he also confessed to murdering 13 years earlier his friend whom he accused of intimacy with his wife. He was executed and his body hung from a gibbet in Knaresborough. His notoriety was romanticised in a ballad by Thomas Hood and in a novel by Bulwer-Lytton.

Ripley

Nearly 200 years ago Ripley, now by-passed by the Harrogate-Ripon road, was a shabby collection of thatched hovels hard by the fortified house which has been the home of the Ingilbys for nearly 700 years. Then Sir William Amcotts Ingilby rebuilt it in solid stone after one in Alsace-Lorraine. Thirty years later Lady Amcotts Ingilby completed the film set, as it were, with a hotel de ville. This is the Ripley you see today, with a cobbled market square, weeping cross and stocks. Its reconstruction was financed by the sale of an outlying farm on which Harrogate is built.

Ripley has some quality shops and a national hyacinth collection and the castle (illustrated), as it is called, is open to the public. There was a settlement "in the territory of the tribe called Hrype" at Domesday. It was reputedly given to the Ingilbys in 1347 when Thomas Ingilby saved Edward III from a charging boar. Soon afterwards the village gained a market and a fair and the Ingilbys fortified their property. Later Capability Brown laid out the deer park. In between, Oliver Cromwell was here. After his triumph at Marston Moor, he billeted his troops in the village and appropriated the castle for himself, much to the distress of Mistress Ingilby who claimed she was ready to shoot him. Bullet scars on the church wall occurred, it is said, in the execution of Royalist prisoners.

The Ingilbys were loyal Roman Catholics and one Sir William Ingilby supported Guy Fawkes in the great gunpowder plot to blow up Parliament. Somehow he managed to escape execution. Ripley is all the more fascinating for me because I once gave an after-dinner speech in the castle to anaesthetists. That is what I call a real challenge.

Silkstone

Pit villages are not the first places you think of to illustrate the quintessential nature of the Yorkshire village. Too much muck. But I was determined to have a pit village – or more likely an ex-pit village – in this book. And bang on cue came Silkstone, west of Barnsley, to my attention. It won the North East regional award in the Daily Telegraph/Calor Gas Village of the Year 2000. "A close knit community which relishes a challenge," said the judges. "The industrial scars of the past are being covered over with grass, flowers and woodland" – to the great credit of its "inexhaustible parish council". Silkstone is no chicken as communities go. The Norman Lord Ilbert de Laci allowed the Saxon Ailric to remain in possession of it at a price after the Conquest. "Silchestone" with its taxable land was duly recorded in Domesday. It seems to have escaped the Norman "Harrying of the North". Its "uncommonly impressive" All Saints parish church, as the authority Niklaus Pevsner described it, with its buttresses and pinnacles, goes back to Norman times but is mostly 15th century.

Not much happened for over 500 years after the Conquest to disturb the even tenor of Silkstone's rural ways until King Charles took refuge in a secret passage at Knabbes Hall to avoid Cromwell's men who, thwarted, set fire to the west wing. Then came the rise of Old King Coal and the tragedy recorded in the churchyard (right). In July 1838, 26 children were drowned trying to get out of Husker Pit flooded by a thunderstorm. Five years later the first union meeting was held in the Ring o' Bells. A century and a half on, Silkstone is energetically in the post-mining clean-up age.

The mortal remains are deposited in the
Graves as undernamed,
1st Grave begining at the North end,
George Birkinshaw Aged 10 Years } Brothers.
Joseph Birkinshaw Aged 7 Years
Isaac Wright Aged 12 Years } Brothers.
Abraham Wright Aged 8 Years
2nd Grave,
James Clarkson Aged 16 Years.
Francis Hoyland Aged 13 Years.
William Atick Aged 12 Years.
Samuel Horne Aged 10 Years.
3rd Grave,
Eli Hutchinson Aged 9 Years.
George Garnett Aged 9 Years.
John Simpson Aged 9 Years.
4th Grave,
George Lamb Aged 8 Years.
William Womersley Aged 8 Years.
James Turton Aged 10 Years.
John Gothard Aged 8 Years.

Wharram Percy

No book of Yorkshire villages is complete without a tribute to those settlements which are no more. Villages do not necessarily last for ever. Some were knocked out in the monastic land rush such as Herleshow because it lay too close to the site of Fountains Abbey. Many others have been absorbed into the West Yorkshire industrial conurbation and other centres of population. But how do you capture what isn't there?

Well, fortunately, there are the remains of Wharram Percy just off the Wolds Way near Wharram Street on the B1248. It is the best-known deserted village site in Britain. It was excavated over 40 years from 1950 and has revolutionised our knowledge of the development of the English village. And there remain an isolated ruined church, with evidence of 12 building phases from the 10th century, and a terrace of 19th century cottages among the earthworks of streets and houses under the control of English Heritage.

Signs of habitation go back to the Neolithic times (3500BC). But the earliest houses excavated were of the Iron Age (100BC). Then came Roman farmsteads, followed by a peasant Saxon or Viking settlement. And by Domesday it had taken the form revealed by the diggings. Percy was added proprietorially by the de Percy family. So why did "the place of the kettle or cauldrons", according to the Old English translation of Wharram, kick the bucket? In essence, poor soil. The village was progressively abandoned over about 200 years until it was finally turned over to sheep in 1500 – and eventually to archaeologists.

Photographic credits

Dorothy Burrows 27, 33 (left), 101 (left), 131, 137
Jacqui Cordingley 113, 133
Chris Craggs 141
Alan Curtis 21, 23, 39, 47, 55, 61 (left), 63, 67, 69, 71, 73, 75, 77, 79, 81, 83, 85, 87, 91, 93, 97
Van Greaves 121
Deryck Hallam 123
Roger Kilvington 129
Mike Kipling 2, 29, 31, 37, 41, 43, 53, 58, 89, 95, 125
Ken Paver 25, 65, 99
Colin Raw 101 (right), 105, 111, 115
David Tarn 5, 10, 49, 51, 57, 59, 61 (right), 103, 139
Simon Warner 94, 107, 109, 117, 119, 127, 135, 143
Keith Watson 13, 16, 33 (right), 35, 45, 50